Sonatinas

Sonatines
Sonatinen

III

K 180

INDEX

Joseph Haydn (1732-1809): 4 Sonaten

Hob. XVI: 8
1.   4

Hob. XVI: 7
2.   8

Hob. XVI: 9
3.   12

Hob. XVI: G1
4.   17

Wolfgang Amadeus Mozart (1756-1791): 6 Sonatines faciles („Wiener Sonatinen")

1. Allegro brillante   22

2. Allegro   30

3. Adagio   38

4. Andante grazioso   42

5. Adagio   48

6. Allegro   52

Ludwig van Beethoven (1770-1827): 2 Sonatinen, Kinsky-Halm Anh. 5

1. Moderato   59

2. Allegro assai   62

4 Sonaten

Joseph Haydn
(1732 - 1809)
Hob. XVI:8

Divertimento

1.

Menuet

Andante

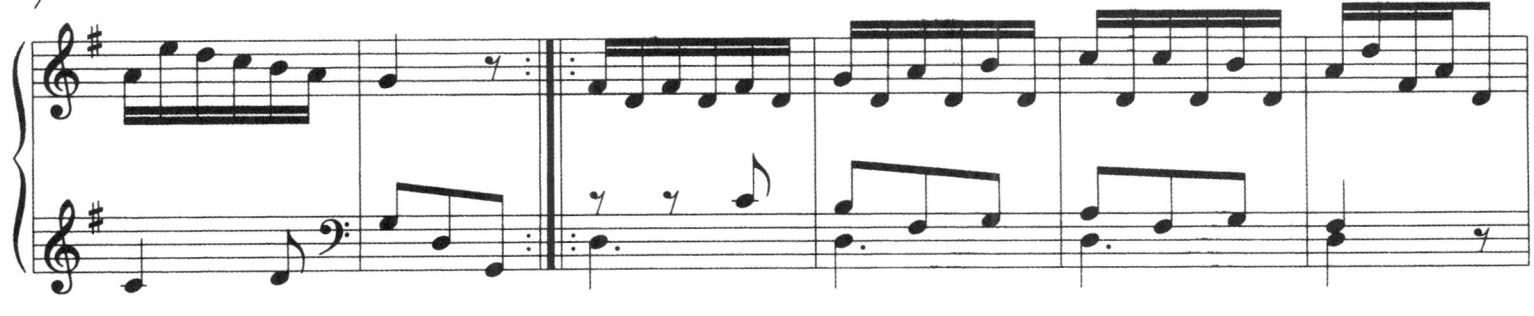

Divertimento
Allegro moderato

Hob. XVI: 7

2.

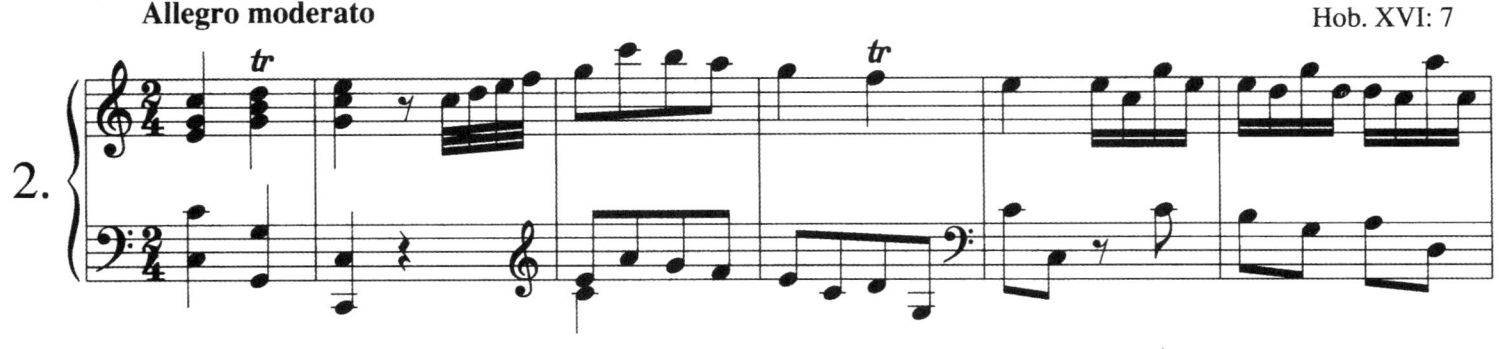

Menuet

Menuet da Capo

Finale
Allegro

10

K 180

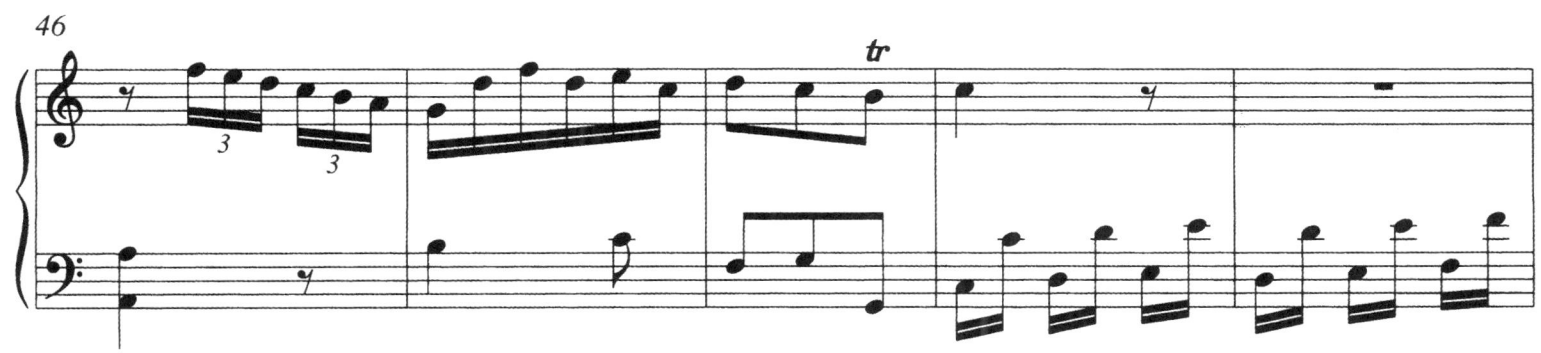

Menuet

Menuet da Capo

Scherzo

Finale
Presto

Da Capo al Segno

6 Sonatines faciles
„Wiener Sonatinen"

Wolfgang Amadeus Mozart
(1756-1791)

Menuetto
Allegretto

Fine

K 180

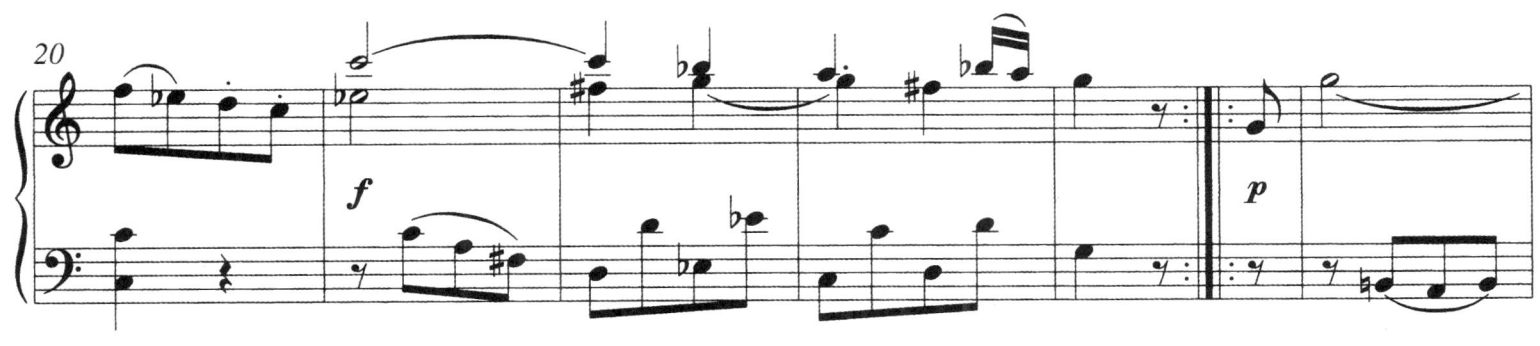

Menuetto
Allegretto

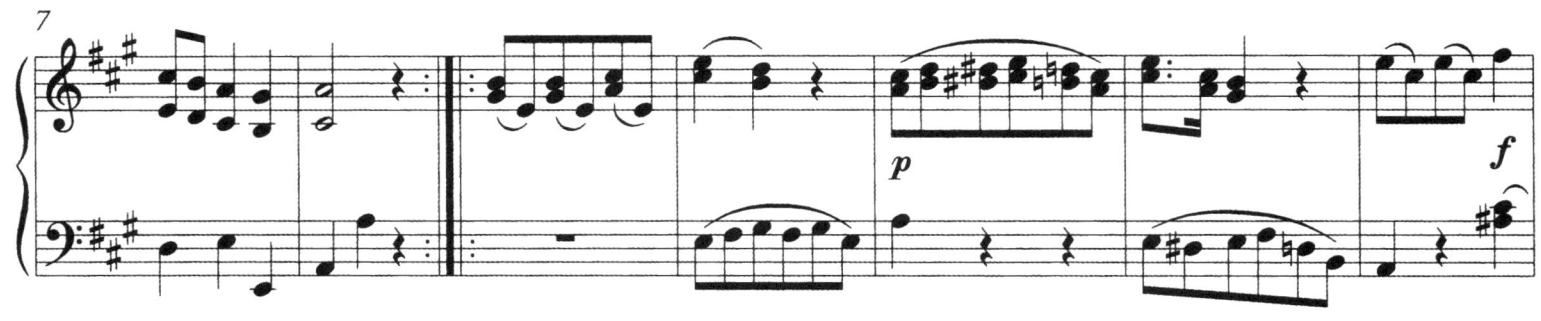
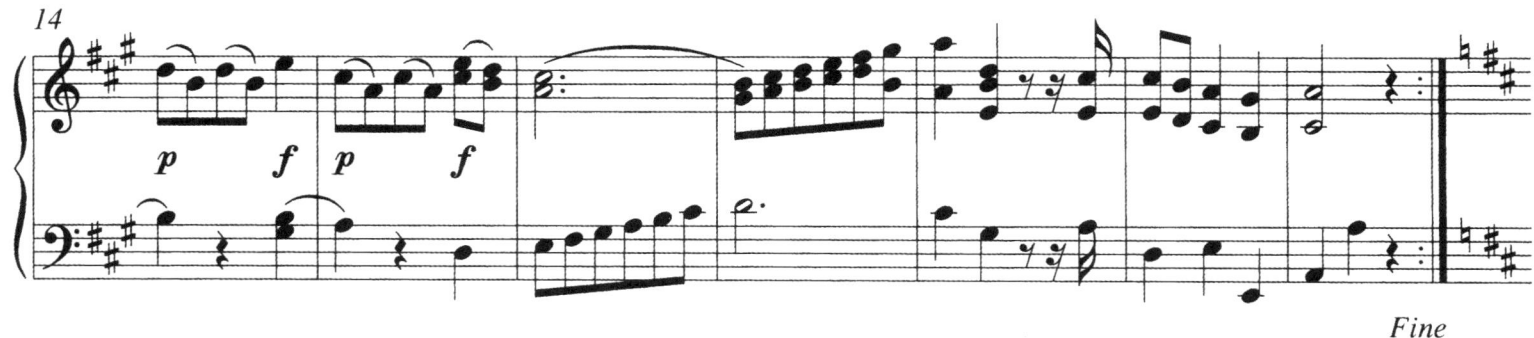

Fine

Trio

Menuetto da Capo

Rondo

K 180

Rondo
Allegro

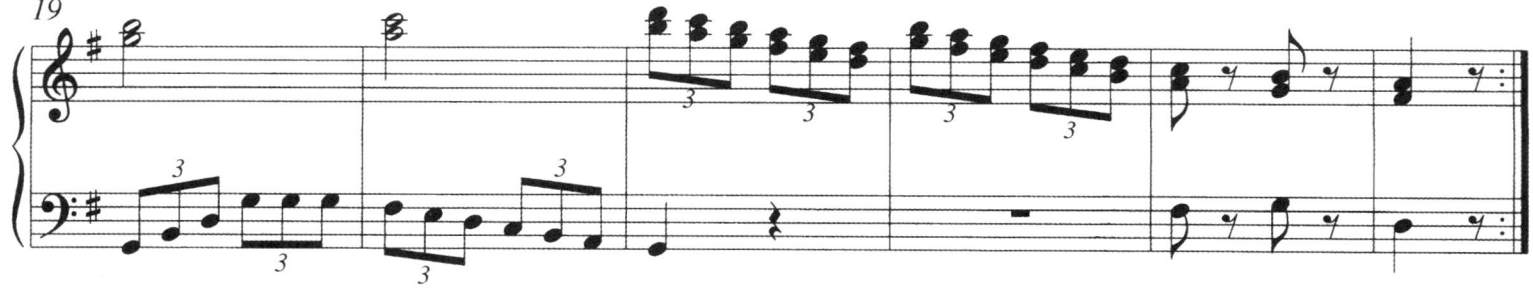

Rondo
Allegro

K 180

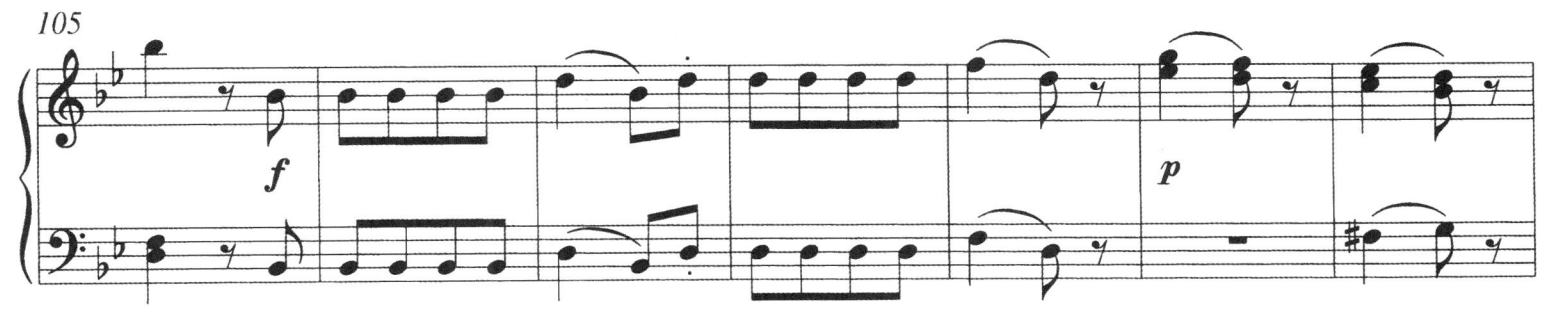

K 180

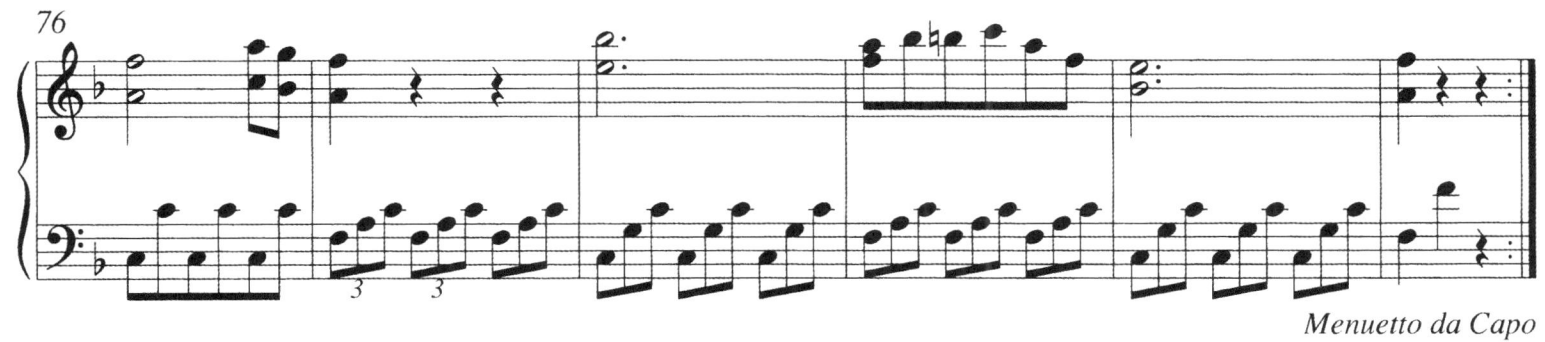

Menuetto da Capo

Polonaise

Finale
Allegro

2 Sonatinen

Ludwig van Beethoven
(1770-1827)
Kinsky-Halm Anh. 5

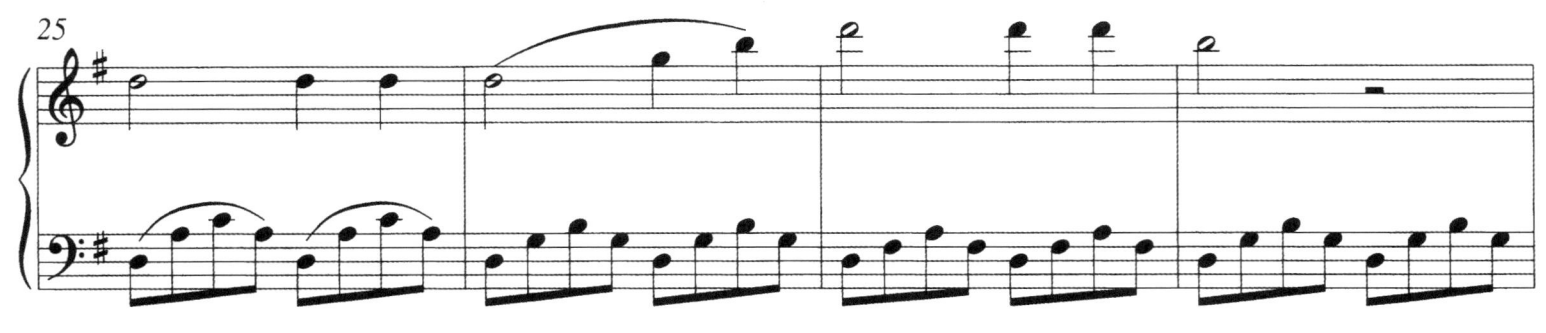

Romanze

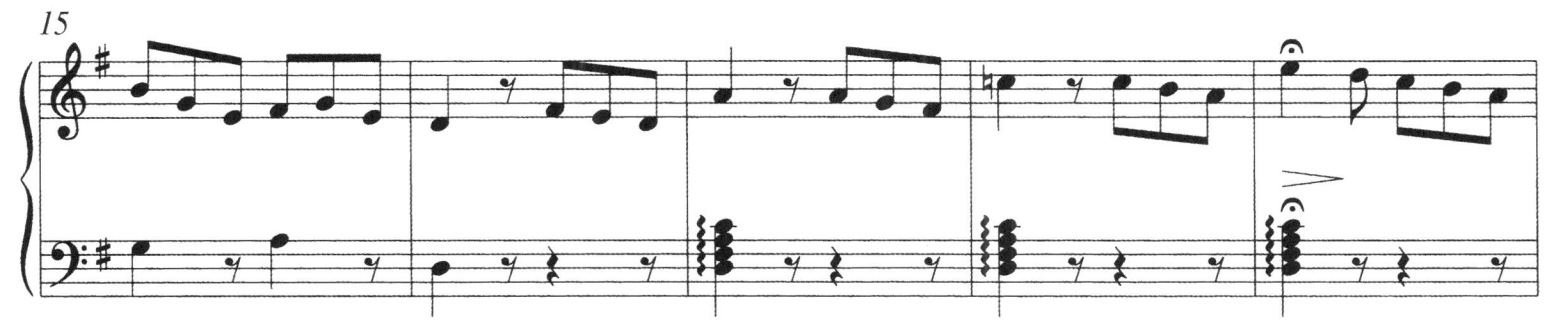

K 180

Rondo
Allegro

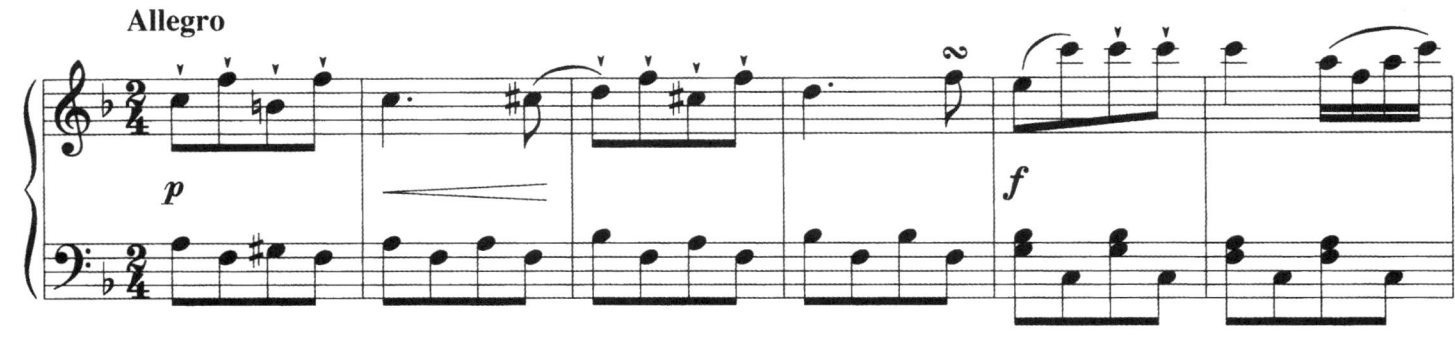
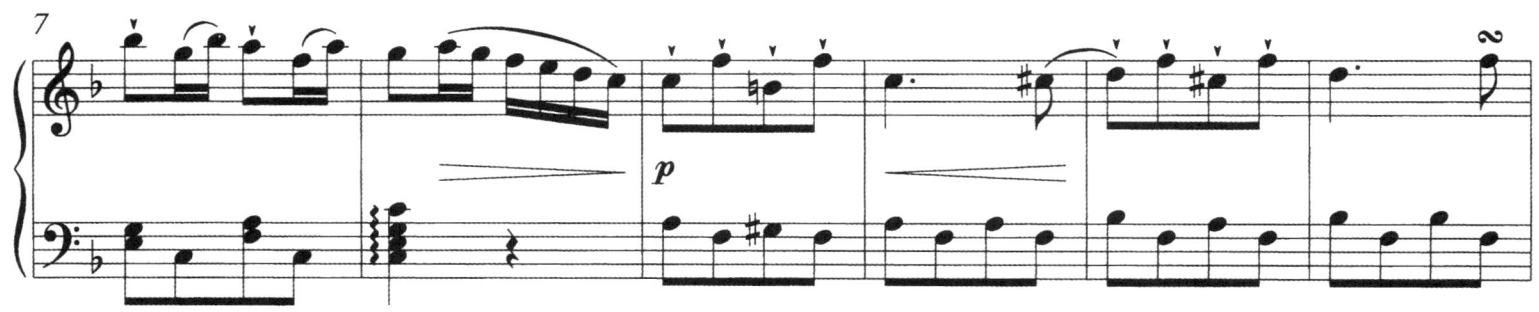

Sonate in C

Ludwig van Beethoven
(1770-1827)
WoO 51

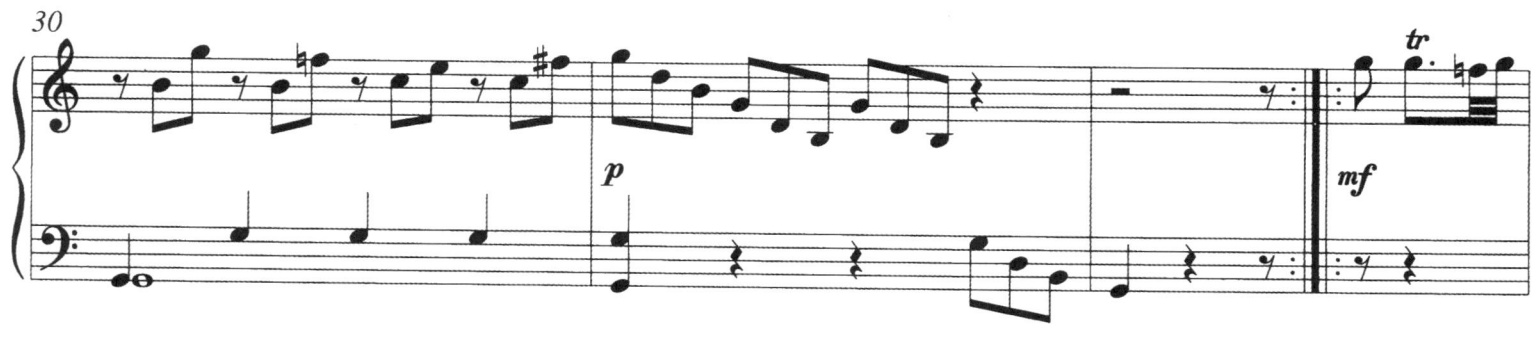

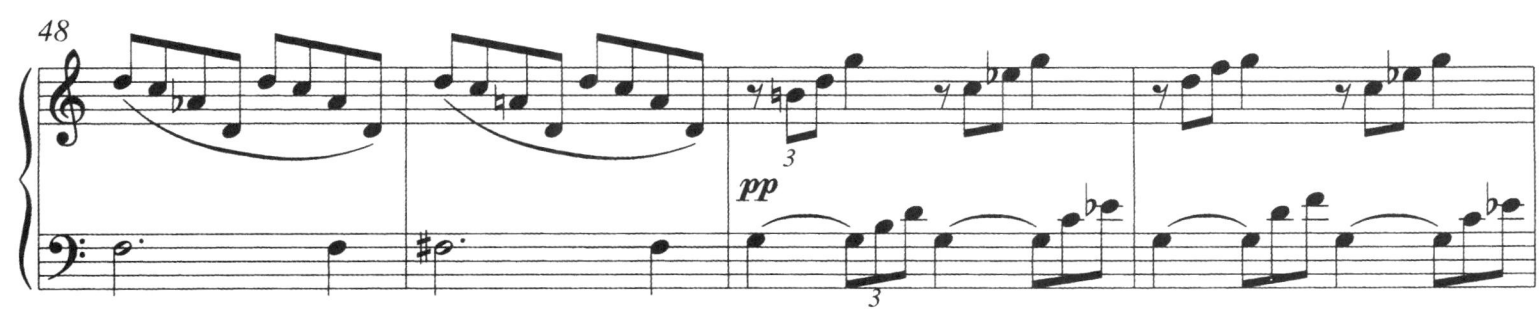

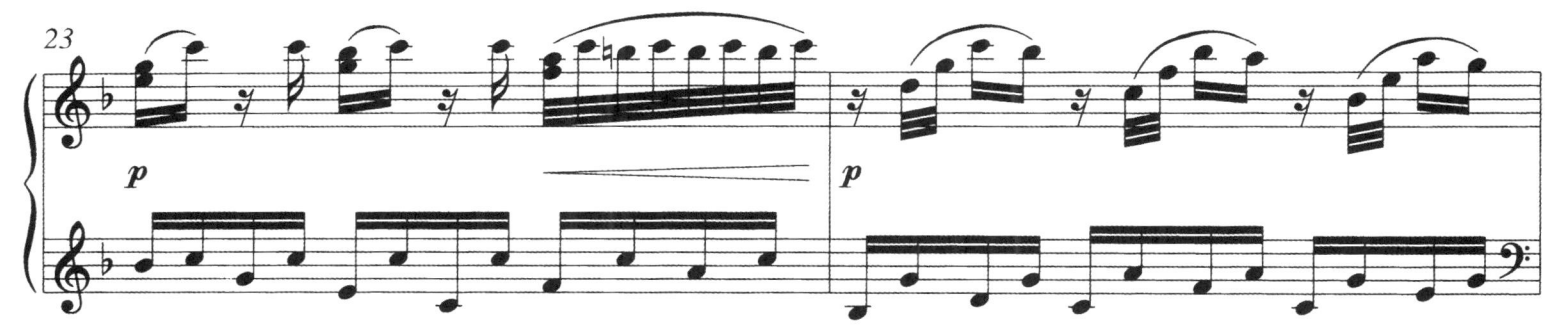

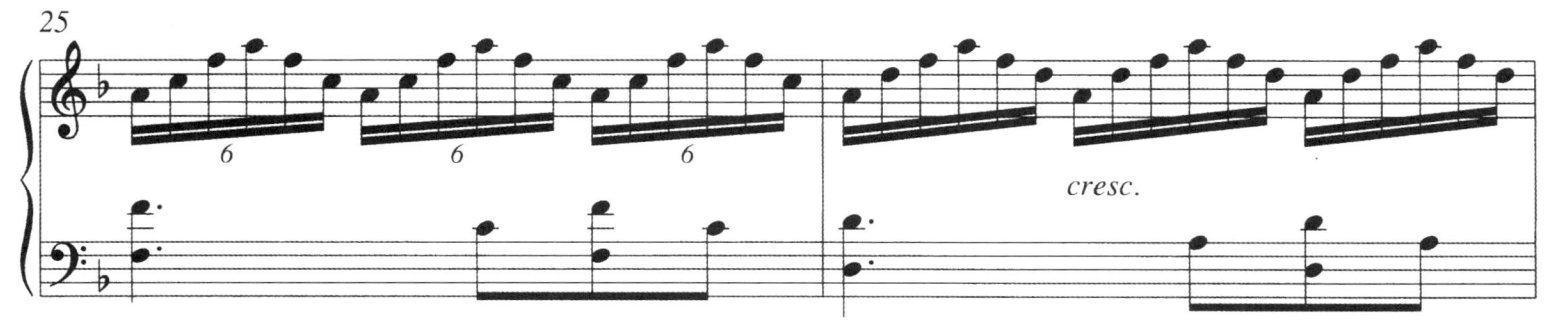
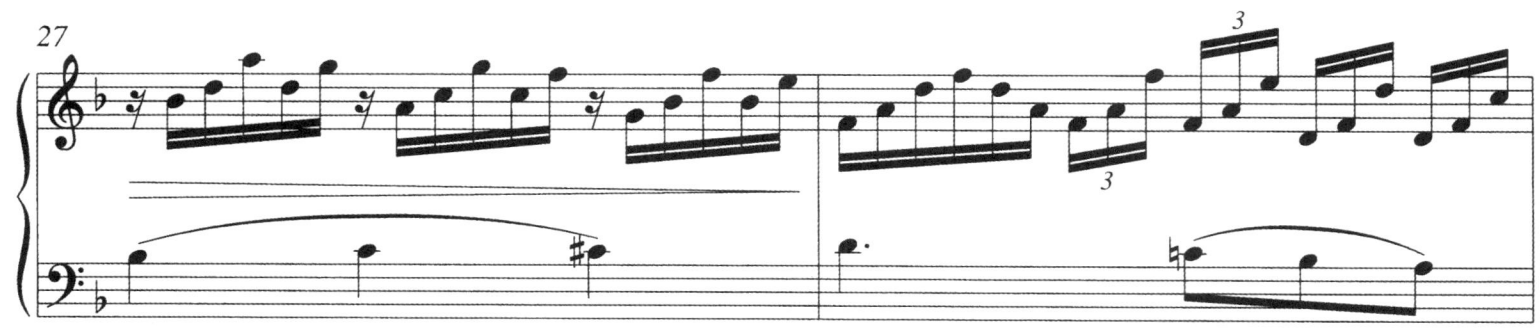

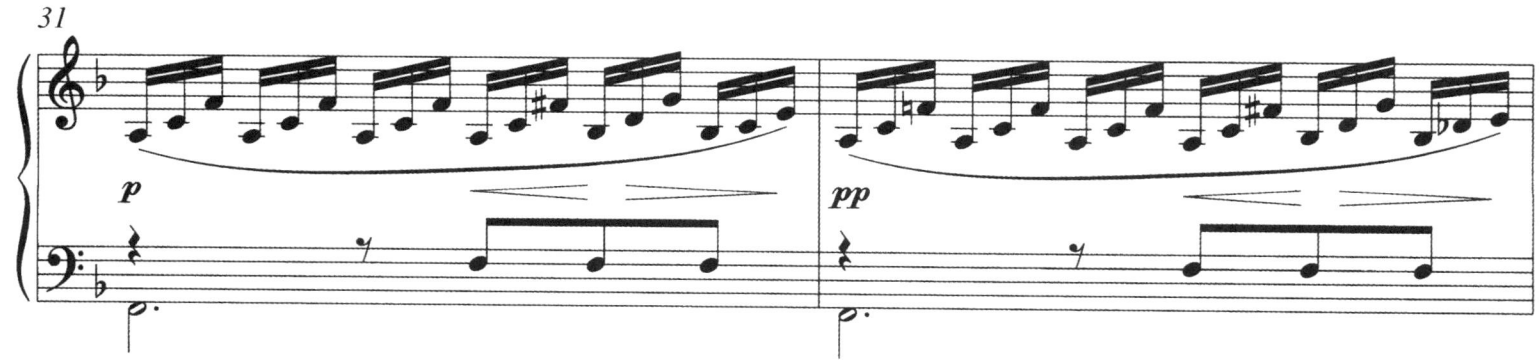

2 Sonates faciles

Ludwig van Beethoven
(1770-1827)
Op. 49, No. 1.

Rondo

Allegro

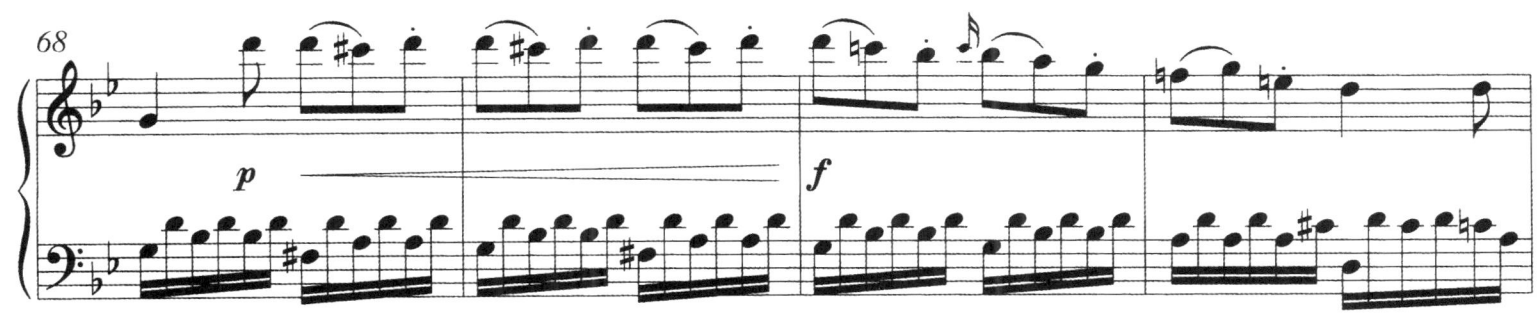

K 180

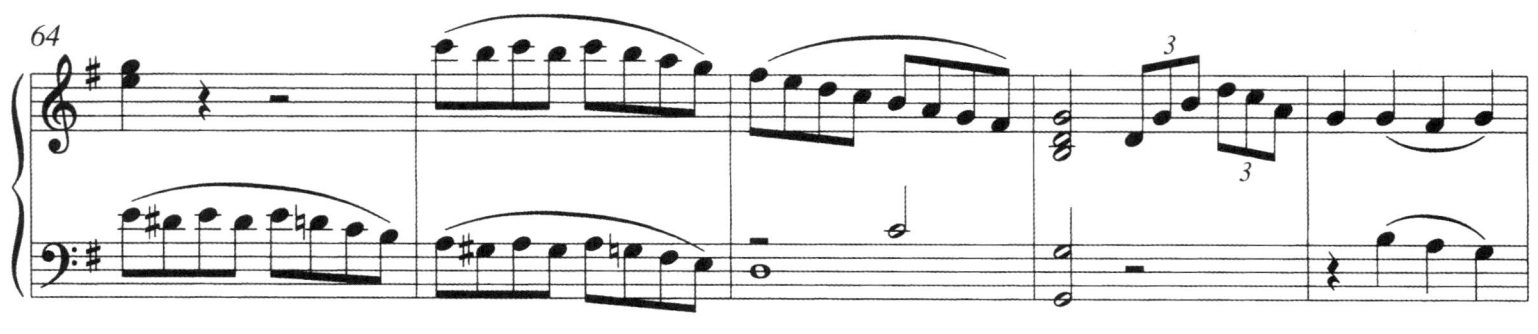

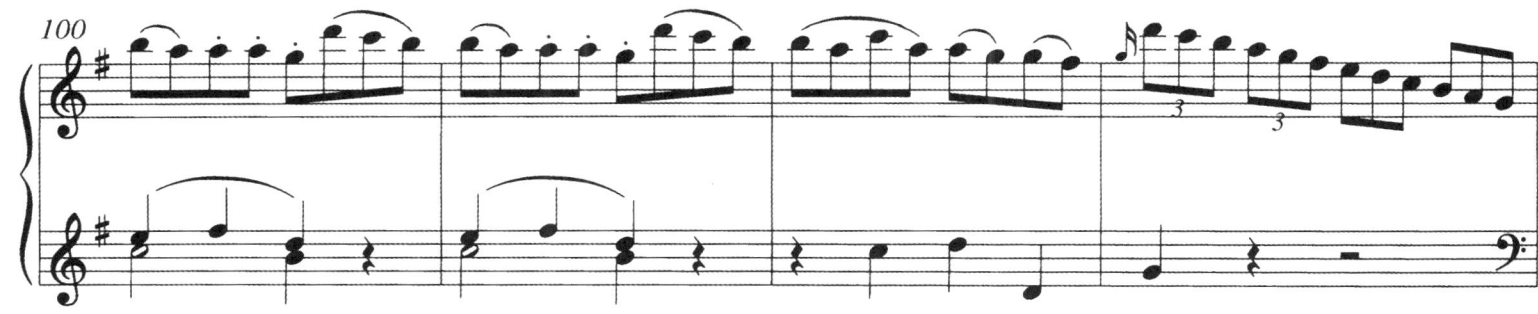

K 180

Tempo di Menuetto

6 Sonatines progressives

Johann Anton André
(1775-1842)
Op. 34

Rondo
Allegretto

Rondo

Allegretto

3.

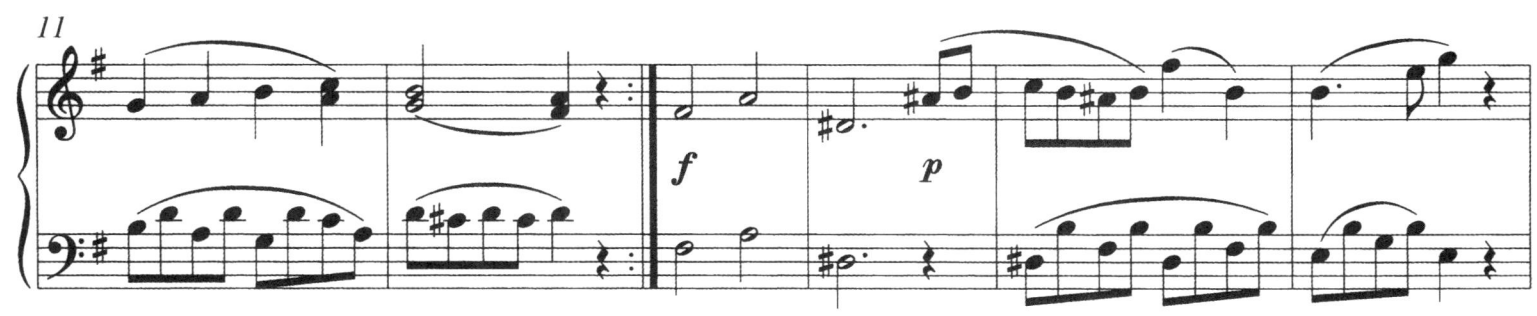

K 180

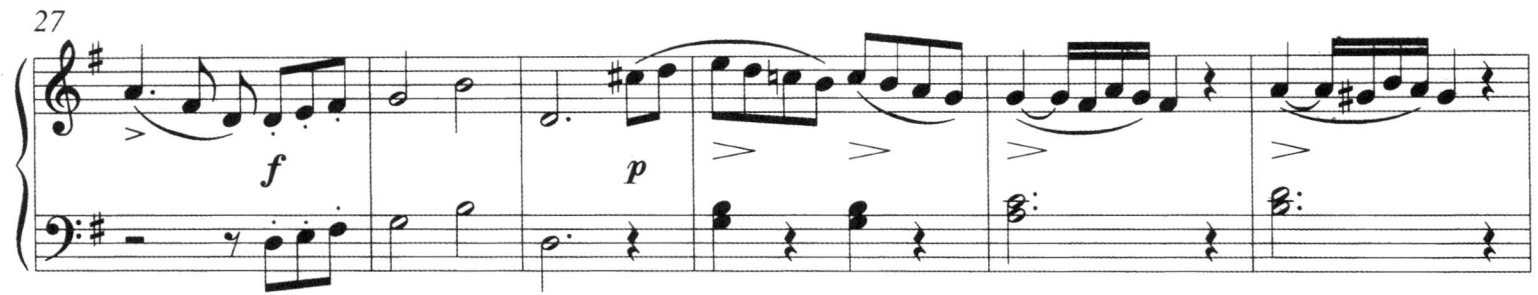

Rondo

Allegretto

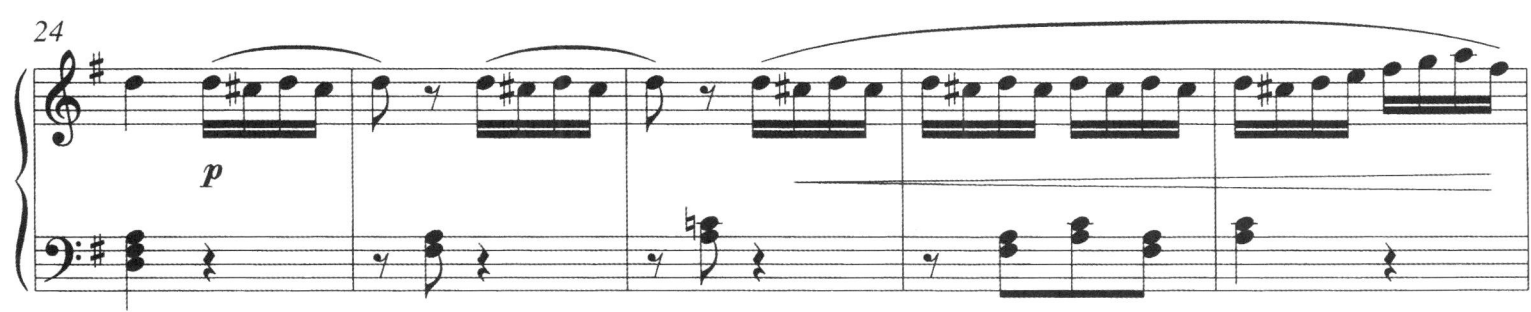

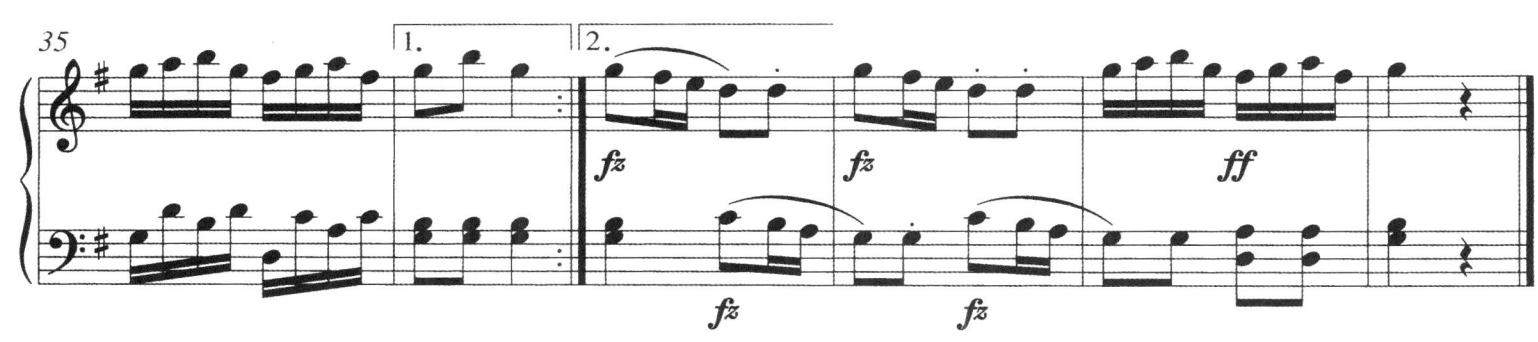

Rondo

Allegretto poco vivace

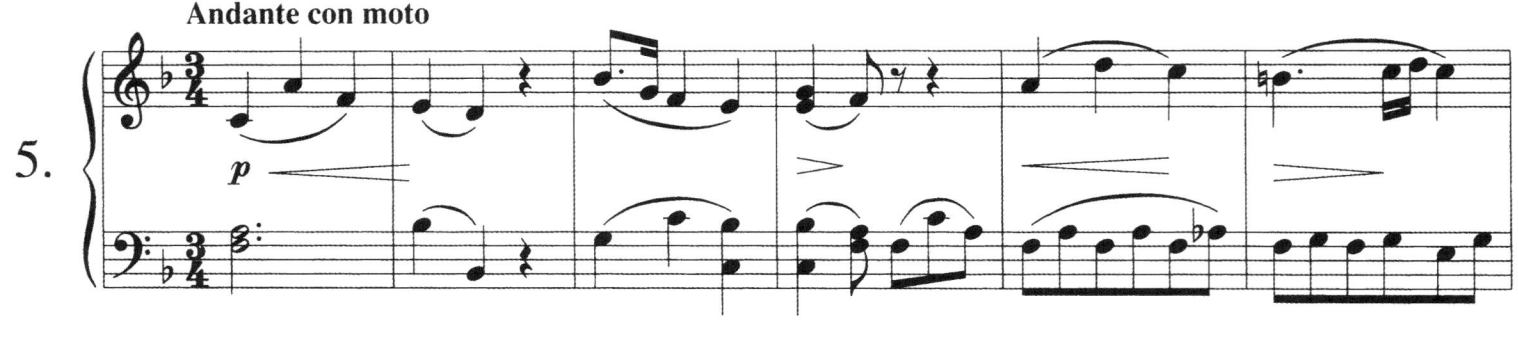

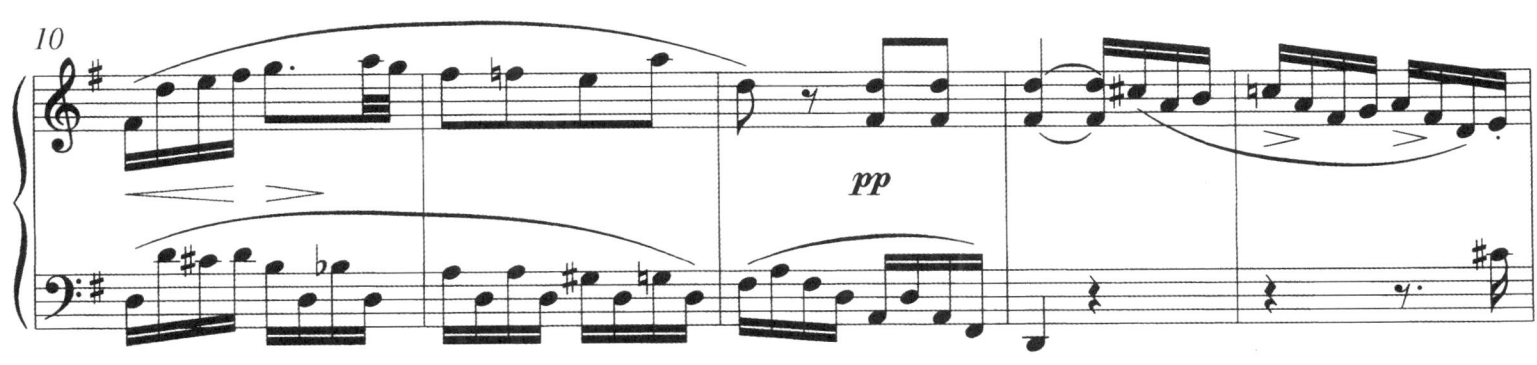

Rondo

4 Sonatinen

Cornelius Gurlitt
(1820-1901)
Op. 214

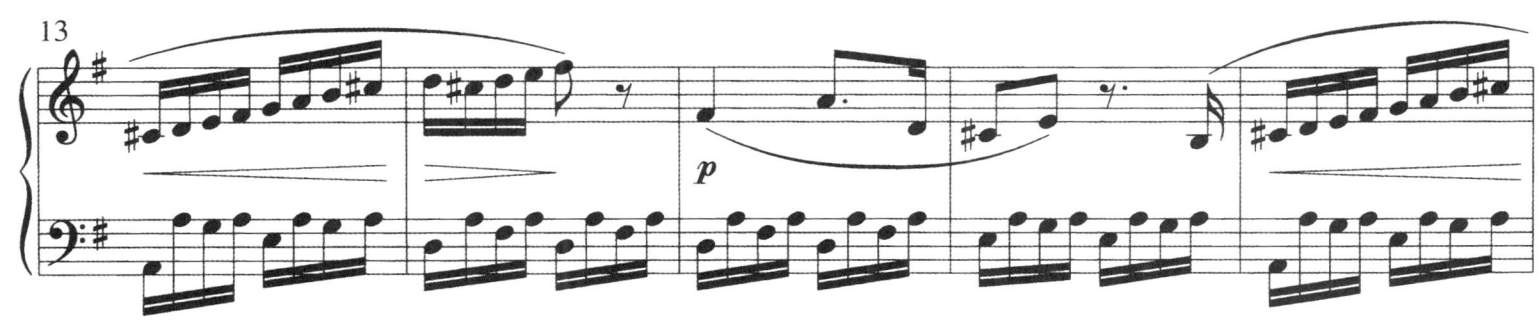

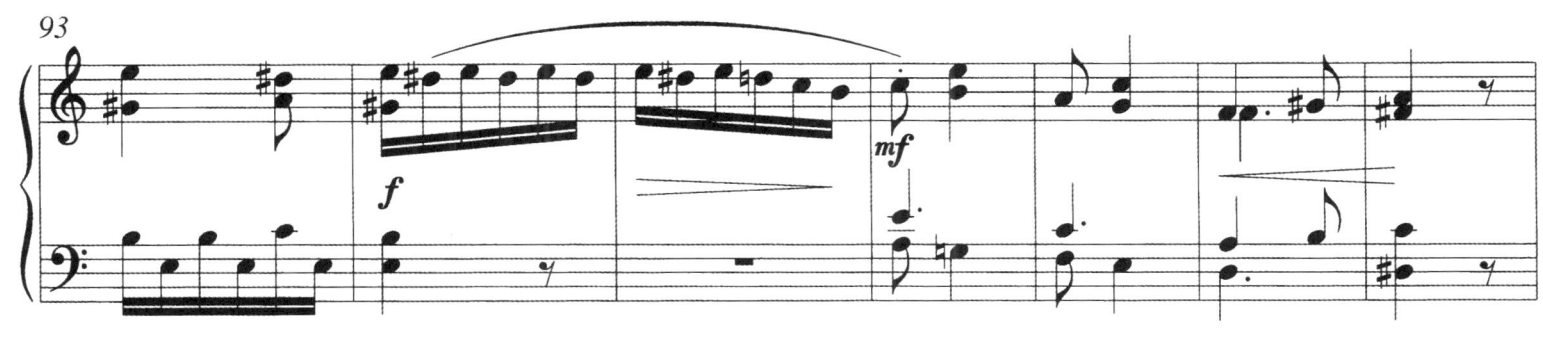

Intermezzo
Andantino

 **MUSICA PIANO**

OVER 25.000 PAGES OF PIANO MUSIC SHEETS ONLINE

Bach, Beethoven, Brahms, Chopin, Czerny, Debussy, Gershwin, Dvořák, Grieg, Haydn, Joplin, Lyadov, Mendelssohn-Bartholdy, Mozart, Mussorgsky, Purcell, Schubert, Schumann, Scriabin, Tchaikovsky and many more

K 180

KÖNEMANN

© 2018 koenemann.com GmbH
www.koenemann.com

Editor: Ágnes Lakos
Responsible co-editors: András Kemenes,
Tamás Zászkaliczky
Technical editor: Desző Varga
Engraved by Kottamester Bt., Budapest

ISBN 978-3-7419-1494-2

Printed in China by Reliance Printing